HOW TO MANAGE STRESS

Life Skills Series
Basic Skills for Lifelong Success

This workbook belongs to:

_____

You may find it helpful to keep important names and phone numbers handy.

Write them below.

Health-care provider

Name_____

Phone_____

Therapist or counselor

Name_____

Phone_____

An emergency contacts

Name_____

Phone_____

Other important numbers

_____
_____
_____
_____
_____
_____
_____
_____
_____
_____
_____
_____
_____
_____
_____
_____

Reentry Essentials, Inc.
98 4th Street, Suite 414
Brooklyn, NY 11231
P: 347.973.0004
E: info@ReentryEssentials.org
I: www.ReentryEssentials.org

© 2019. Reentry Essentials, Inc. All rights reserved. No part of the material protected by this copyright may be reproduced or used in any form or by any means, electronic or mechanical, including photocopying, recording or by information storage and retrieval system without written permission from the copyright owner.

FEELING STRESSED?

If so, this workbook can help you understand stress—what causes it and how you can manage it.

Friends and family members can be a wonderful source of support. Share your thoughts and feelings with them. Brainstorm together for ways to reduce stress.

Some stress will always be a part of your life. You can learn to manage it better, become more productive and enjoy the challenges life throws your way.

CONTENT

What is stress?	3
Stress can take its toll on you.	4
What are your "warning signals"?	5
What's causing all that stress?	7
Keeping a journal	9
You can stop contributing to your stress	13
How do you respond to stressors?	14
Are you hearing negative self-talk?	15
Positive thinking can help	16
Tips for reducing stress	17
Learn to better manage your time.	18
Make time for free time.	19
How are you spending your time?	20
Take a look at your lifestyle.	21
Good nutrition makes good sense.	23
Try relaxing your body and mind.	24
Consider one or more of these relaxation techniques:	25
Alcohol and other drugs won't help.	27
Asking for help is not a sign of weakness.	28
Developing a stress management plan	29

WHAT IS STRESS?

Stress is sometimes referred to as the "pressure" or "tension" you feel when faced with a situation that's new, unpleasant or threatening.

Stress is a fact of life.

It affects everyone. Some stress is actually helpful because it can spur you to meet life's challenges. Without some stress, life would be boring.

Stress can be an automatic reaction to a demand or danger.

Your muscles tense and your heart rate and breathing speed up. A rush of adrenaline gives you the strength and energy needed to deal with danger or run away. This reaction is often called the "fight-or-flight" response.

Too much stress can cause problems.

It can affect your mental and physical health and damage relationships with friends and family.

STRESS CAN TAKE ITS TOLL ON YOU.
Unless you take steps to reduce or control stress, tension can build up inside.

Over time, stress can harm your health, possibly contributing to:

- allergies
- muscle tension, often in the form of a stiff neck or sore back
- upset stomach or heartburn
- sore throats, sinus infections, colds and flu
- migraine or tension headaches
- sleep disorders
- menstrual irregularity
- high blood pressure
- angina
- heart disease and heart attacks
- stroke (brain attack)

If you already have any of the conditions listed above, don't just assume stress is to blame. Talk to your health-care provider.

Poor health can lead to more stress, making your problems even worse.

For example:

- living with chronic pain, such as pain caused by a back problem, may make you feel frustrated and alone
- missing important events due to colds and flu may cause anxiety

If you have an untreated health problem, see your health-care provider right away. Once a problem has been diagnosed, be sure to follow your health-care provider's directions for treating it. A positive attitude and improved health will help you handle stress.

WHAT ARE YOUR "WARNING SIGNALS"?

You'll be better able to manage stress if you recognize the symptoms. Check the symptoms you frequently feel when you're stressed. Add any symptoms you've experienced repeatedly that aren't listed. Please note that some of the symptoms listed below also have causes other than stress. See your health-care provider if symptoms are severe or persistent.

You'll be better able to manage stress if you recognize the symptoms. Check the symptoms you frequently feel when you're stressed. Add any symptoms you've experienced repeatedly that aren't listed. Please note that some of the symptoms listed below also have causes other than stress. See your health-care provider if symptoms are severe or persistent.

Physical symptoms:

☐ a change in appetite
☐ back pain
☐ high blood pressure
☐ breathlessness
☐ chest pain
☐ clammy hands
☐ a cold
☐ constipation or diarrhea
☐ fatigue
☐ headaches
☐ racing heartbeat
☐ jaw clenching and/ or grinding of teeth
☐ muscle tension
☐ rashes
☐ restlessness
☐ sleeping problems
☐ stomachaches

Other physical symptoms:

_____
_____
_____
_____
_____
_____
_____
_____
_____
_____
_____
_____
_____
_____
_____
_____
_____
_____

Emotional symptoms:

- ☐ anger
- ☐ anxiety
- ☐ denial of a problem
- ☐ depression
- ☐ forgetfulness
- ☐ difficulty making decisions
- ☐ feeling powerless
- ☐ feeling rejected
- ☐ feeling unhappy for no reason
- ☐ being easily upset
- ☐ worrying frequently
- ☐ feeling worthless.

Behavioral symptoms:

- ☐ arguing with friends or partner
- ☐ avoiding tasks and responsibilities
- ☐ crying easily
- ☐ decreased job performance
- ☐ difficulty concentrating
- ☐ increasing use of alcohol, tobacco or other drugs
- ☐ neglecting appearance
- ☐ overeating or underrating
- ☐ snapping at people withdrawing from family and friends

Notes:
_____

Other emotional symptoms:
_____

Other behavioral symptoms:
_____

WHAT'S CAUSING ALL THAT STRESS?

Some people don't know—they're too busy and too stressed to stop and think about why they feel that way. But by recognizing the sources of stress, called stressors, you may be able to make changes and reduce stress.

Everyone's stressors are different.

What's stressful for one person may not bother someone else at all. For example, you may feel stressed by caring for an aging parent, but a sibling may enjoy it.

Not all stressors are bad.

For example, a sudden financial gain can also create stress.

Read the following lists of potential stressors. Check the ones that are stressful for you. Feel free to add other stressors to the list. (You may want to consider making your biggest stressors part of your stress management plan. See pages 29 and 30.)

Financial stressors:
- ☐ alimony
- ☐ bankruptcy
- ☐ child support
- ☐ growing debts
- ☐ sudden financial gain
- ☐ fixed income
- ☐ reduced income due to retirement
- ☐ taxes
- ☐ _____

Daily hassles:
- ☐ car trouble
- ☐ child care
- ☐ household chores
- ☐ forgetting or misplacing something
- ☐ oversleeping
- ☐ traffic jams
- ☐ waiting in lines
- ☐ _____

Environmental stressors:
- ☐ crime
- ☐ noise
- ☐ overcrowding
- ☐ pollution
- ☐ traffic
- ☐ weather
- ☐ _____

Health-related stressors:
- ☐ arthritis
- ☐ poor eyesight
- ☐ poor hearing
- ☐ headaches
- ☐ illness, injury or disease
- ☐ trouble with medicines
- ☐ loss of mobility
- ☐ being overweight
- ☐ chronic pain
- ☐ sleep disorders
- ☐ _____

Family-related stressors:
- ☐ arguments with partner or children
- ☐ a child moving out or returning home
- ☐ poor communication between family members
- ☐ the death of a family member or partner
- ☐ divorce or separation
- ☐ alcohol or other drug problems (self or other
- ☐ helping an older relative
- ☐ serious illness, injury or surgery
- ☐ problems with in-laws or other relatives
- ☐ marriage
- ☐ moving
- ☐ parenting challenges
- ☐ pregnancy or adoption
- ☐ sexual problems with partner
- ☐ being single or alone
- ☐ _____

Work-related stressors:
- ☐ a business move or merger; downsizing
- ☐ a long commute
- ☐ being fired or laid off
- ☐ a noisy or unpleasant work environment
- ☐ few opportunistic advancement
- ☐ little recognition or a lack of feedback
- ☐ new responsibilities
- ☐ retirement
- ☐ starting a new job or getting a promotion
- ☐ a lack of training
- ☐ trouble with a boss or co-workers
- ☐ too much wore
- ☐ _____

KEEPING A JOURNAL
can help you manage stress.

Keeping a journal has many benefits.

It can be:

- a tool to help you see what causes you stress and how it affects you
- an outlet for emotion and frustration
- a decision-making tool, allowing you to explore pros and cons of possible choices
- a helpful way to confront problems or make a change in your life
- a fun activity, because you don't have to follow any rules
- a way to gain insights, because you may discover solutions to a problem or find ways to change stressful situations

Try it out.

Each day this week, write about something that made you feel stressed—or that made you feel good. If you need help getting started, try answering some of these questions:

- How did you respond to a stressful situation today?
- Did you laugh today? At what?
- Are you facing any big decisions? Explain them.
- Are you feeling anxious or frustrated? Why?

Today's date is _____

_____
_____
_____
_____
_____
_____
_____
_____
_____
_____
_____
_____

Today's date is _____

Today's date is _____

Today's date is _____

_____
_____
_____
_____
_____
_____
_____
_____
_____
_____
_____
_____

Today's date is _____

_____
_____
_____
_____
_____
_____
_____
_____
_____
_____
_____
_____

Today's date is _____

Today's date is _____

YOU CAN STOP CONTRIBUTING TO YOUR STRESS.

Some people have certain personality traits that help them overcome stress—optimism, a tendency to take action and a sense of humor. You can develop these traits—and stop adding to your stress.

Accept what you cannot change. Be optimistic.

Many people worry about things they have no control over. To manage stress, you need to learn to accept things you cannot change and be optimistic about the outcome. For example, imagine your company has just purchased machines you don't know how to use. Worrying about it will only increase your stress. Instead, think about getting the training you need to use them.

When you can't change a situation, be optimistic.

Try thinking:

- "I'll laugh about this someday."
- "Maybe some good will come of this."
- "What can I learn from this?"

By focusing on something positive, you can discover solutions to problems and feel less stress.

Exercise control over what you can change.

Rather than feel stressed by something you can control, take action! Change the situation.

For example, if your job is causing you too much stress, consider finding another one.

Cope with stress through humor. Be playful.

Laughter not only makes you feel good, it can also help you relax. Look for the silly and absurd activities going on around you, and learn to laugh at them. By taking things a little less seriously and adding laughter to your life, you can better control stress.

HOW DO YOU RESPOND TO STRESSORS?

Look back at the lists of stressors on pages 7 and 8. List the 3 stressors that bother you the most.

1. _____ 2. _____ 3. _____

Describe a situation you recently experienced involving each of these 3 stressors. How did you react? How could you react to a similar situation in the future so you would feel less stress?

Situation	Initial reaction	Possible change
Bills were piling up, and I didn't have enough money to pay them all.	Felt overwhelmed and stressed. Was convinced I'd never get out of debt.	Explain the problem to my creditors, and ask for more time to pay. Set a budget, and stick to it.

1. _____
_____
_____
_____

2. _____
_____
_____
_____

3. _____
_____
_____
_____

When confronted with a stressor in the future, stop for a moment and think about how to react. Can you control this stressor? Think about how to react to it in a positive way that can give you more control!

ARE YOU HEARING NEGATIVE SELF-TALK?

Whether you're conscious of it or not, you probably talk to yourself silently every day. This mental conversation is called self-talk.

Negative self-talk "loops"

Unfortunately, we often criticize ourselves during these mental conversations, turning a minor fault or problem into a big one. These "loops" replay themselves in our heads, reinforcing negative (and incorrect) beliefs. They can also add to our stress—it's our self-talk that helps determine how we will respond to any situation.

Recording a new loop

Every time you hear a negative message play in your mind, erase it and record a new, positive one in its place.

For example, instead of saying, I'll never be any good at making speeches," try saying, I'll just keep practicing and do my best. No one expects me to be perfect."

Or, instead of saying, "I know I'll probably be fired and never find another job" when you're stuck in traffic and late for work, try saying, "This happens to everyone. I'll get there as soon as I can."

By learning to identify, challenge and change negative messages, you can reduce stress.

POSITIVE THINKING CAN HELP.

Using the space below, write down several stressful situations you've recently faced. Did you hear a negative message? What positive message could you "play" when you face the situation again?

Situation	Negative message	Positive message
1.	1.	1.
2.	2.	2.
3.	3.	3.
4.	4.	4.

The next time you face a potentially stressful situation, stop and listen to the loop playing in your head. Does it have a negative message? Try to change the message to a positive one. Over time, your mind will automatically play the new, positive messages, making it easier for you to manage stress.

TIPS FOR REDUCING STRESS

These tips can be adapted to a variety of situations— college life, parenthood, volunteer activities, the workplace, and so forth.

Get up on time

So you aren't rushed.

Designate a time and place to do your work

—and leave it there. For example, a college student could study at the library and leave work in a locker.

Understand what's expected

Before starting a project. It might not be as overwhelming as it seems.

Minimize interruptions,

Especially if you need to concentrate. Close the door or don't answer the phone.

Get help

When needed, or delegate less important chores and tasks. For example, ask children to set the table or help with housework. By doing so, you'll be better able to focus on your priorities.

Get organized

So you can find things quickly. Remind yourself of your accomplishments rather than concentrating only on what hasn't been done. Doing so will help motivate you.

Alternate mental and physical tasks,

if possible, to save energy and reduce fatigue.

Look positively at change, instead of fearing it.

While change may bring challenges, it may also bring many benefits you don't expect. For example, moving to a new town may be scary, but you'll make new friends.

Look back on a crisis

As a learning opportunity. This will help you respond better to similar problems in the future.

LEARN TO BETTER MANAGE YOUR TIME.

Poor use of time, not a lack of time, may be contributing to your stress level. Here are some tips for handling almost any situation.

Plan ahead

by determining when a task must be finished and how much time it will take. Overestimate how long it will take to finish jobs, such as a term paper or a report for work, especially if you haven't done them before.

Break big jobs down

Into small chunks. They will seem more manageable, and you'll feel a sense of accomplishment as you finish each part.

Determine priorities

And spend your time on the most important activities. For example, spending time with your family may be more important than keeping your home spotless.

Look for ways to be more efficient.

Such as cooking several meals at once and refrigerating them for the week ahead.

Take breaks periodically

You'll work more efficiently when you return to a project.

Group similar tasks

Do them at the same time. For example, make all of your phone calls at once or pay all of your bills at the same time.

Schedule work

Based on your energy level. Work on more difficult tasks when you generally have the most energy for example, first thing in the morning or after lunch.

MAKE TIME FOR FREE TIME.

Poor use of time, not a lack of time, may be contributing to your stress level. Here are some tips for handling almost any situation.

Include yourself in your schedule.

Don't think of free time as what's left over after you've done everything else. Along with scheduling your work responsibilities and family commitments, plan time to exercise, read, rake a bubble bath or do anything else you find relaxing. Making time for things you enjoy will help you "recharge your batteries."

Learn to say no.

Saying no to another volunteer activity, an optional presentation at work or even a social event can give you more free time or more time to devote to other responsibilities.

Don't feel guilty when you say no. It's not always easy, but with practice, you can learn.

LIFE SKILLS SERIES: BASIC SKILLS FOR LIFELONG SUCCESS   HOW TO MANAGE STRESS

HOW ARE YOU SPENDING YOUR TIME?

Writing down your activities for a week or even a month is one of the best ways to see where you're wasting time. It can also help you see where you can schedule free time and how to become more efficient month is one of the best ways to see where you're wasting time. It can also help you see where you can schedule free time and how to become more efficient.

Using the chart below, or one like it, note how you spend your time. Note time spent at work, shopping, talking on the phone, commuting, watching TV or making dinner.

Day	Activity	Time Spent

Review your chart, and answer the following questions:

- Are there tasks that could have been delegated?
- Could you have done anything more efficiently?
- Are you getting enough time for your favorite activities?

Try changing your schedule so that it is more realistic, gives you free time and reduces stress.

TAKE A LOOK AT YOUR LIFESTYLE.
In addition to changing your reaction to stressors, consider:

Seeing your healthcare provider
Have regular checkups. Talk to your health-care provider about stress and how it affects you.

Talking it over
Talking with a friend or family member can help you son out your feelings and get a new perspective on problems.

Getting plenty of sleep
Most adults need 7-9 hours of sleep each night. Often, people under stress give up sleep to finish more work. Others can't sleep because they're thinking about their stress. If you have trouble sleeping:

- Exercise during the day.
- Don't drink alcohol or caffeinated beverages in the evening. They can keep you awake.
- Take a warm bath before going to bed.
- Go to bed at the same time every night.
- Write about your worries in a journal, or mentally set them aside. Plan to think about them another time.

Getting enough physical activity
The key is to find a health balance between the calories you eat and those you bum.

- Get at least 150 minutes of moderate—or 75 minutes of vigorous physical activity each week.
- For greater health benefits, get at least 300 minutes of moderate—or 150 minutes of vigorous physical activity each week.
- Try to spread your activity throughout the week, getting at least 10 minutes at a time.
- In addition, do muscle strengthening exercises at least 2 days each week.

Be sure to consult your healthcare provider before starting or changing an exercise program.

Exercise levels
- Moderate activity is any activity that increases your heart and breathing rates—but still allows you to carry on a conversation without difficulty.
- Vigorous activity is any activity that increases your heart and breathing rates to the point that conversation is difficult or broken.

Taking a break

A relaxing activity can revitalize you and boost your spirits. Afterward, you'll have more emotional strength to face challenges.

Avoiding stress

Too many major changes at once can lead to tension. Deal with a few stressful events before working on others.

Taking up a new hobby

Hobbies can take your mind off your problems, help you relax and increase your self-esteem.

Listening to music

Quiet, soothing music, alone or with the relaxation techniques on pages 25 and 26, may help you relax.

"Treating" yourself

Find something to look forward to, such as eating lunch outside or going for a short walk.

Watching what you eat

An unhealthy diet can lead to problems that may add to your stress. The tips on the next page will give you a good start to creating a healthy diet.

List any other stress-reducing techniques you think of:
_____
_____
_____

Which stress-reducing techniques do you think will work best for you? Write them below.
_____
_____
_____

Not every technique will work for everyone. Try different techniques to see which ones work best for you. Remember—changing behavior takes time, so stick with it!

GOOD NUTRITION MAKES GOOD SENSE.
Your body needs extra energy when you're under stress.
Pay special attention to what you eat—and what you don't eat.

Don't skip breakfast.

Your body needs energy after 8-12 hours without food. Skipping breakfast can make you feel tired and cause headaches.

Eat for good health.

No single meal will make or break your health. But consistently making healthier choices can help you maintain a healthy weight and lower your risk for chronic diseases.

- Make a variety of nutrient dense choices from each food group in the right amounts for your calorie needs.
- Vary your choices from each food group over the week.
- Make small shifts to healthier choices. For example, switch to fat-free or low-fat dairy products. Choose seafood, lean meats, lean poultry, nuts, seeds and soy products over, high-fat meats.

Cut back on caffeine.

Caffeine, which is found in coffee, tea, soft drinks and chocolate, is a stimulant. It can worsen the impact of stress on your body. Ask your healthcare provider if there is caffeine in the medicines you cake.

Stick to a regular meal schedule.

Skipping meals or eating at irregular times can lower your energy level.

Don't overeat.

Many people turn to food when they are under stress. However, overeating can lead to weight gain and other stressful health problems.

Your body needs extra energy when you're under stress. Pay special attention to what you eat and what you don't eat

For more information on nutrition, or to tailor a diet to meet your needs, talk to a dietitian, nutritionist or your health-care provider.

You can also visit www.ChooseMyPlate.gov.

TRY RELAXING YOUR BODY AND MIND.

The relaxation techniques on pages 25-26 will not only help you manage stress, but they can also improve your concentration, productivity and overall well-being. To get started:

Find a quiet, relaxing place.

Where you will be alone for 10-20 minutes, to do these exercises. The techniques work best if there are no distractions.

Practice once or twice a day,

at whatever time works best for you. (Some people practice before breakfast to ease into the day, while others practice after work to unwind.)

Stick with the technique that works best

For you. Not every technique will work for every person.

Keep trying

Don't worry if you don't notice a major change immediately. You may need to practice for a few weeks before you begin to feel the benefits. Remember, you should see your healthcare provider if symptoms of stress are severe or persist.

CONSIDER ONE OR MORE OF THESE RELAXATION TECHNIQUES:

Progressive muscle relaxation

This technique can help you relax the major muscle groups in your body. And, it's easy to do.

1. Wear loose, comfortable clothing. Sit in a favorite chair or lie down.
2. Begin with your facial muscles. Frown hard for 5-10 seconds and then relax all your muscles.
3. Work other facial muscles by scrunching your face up or knitting your eyebrows for
4. 5-10 seconds. Release. You should feel a noticeable difference between the tense and relaxed muscles.
5. Move on to your jaw. Then, move on to other muscle groups—shoulders, arms, chest and legs- until you've tensed and relaxed your whole body.

Visualization

This technique uses your imagination, a great resource when it comes to reducing stress.

1. Sit or lie down in a comfortable position.
2. Imagine a pleasant, peaceful scene, such as a lush forest or a sandy beach. Picture yourself in this setting.
3. Focus on the scene for a set amount of time, then gradually return to your other activities.

Meditation

This is the process of focusing on a single word or object to clear your mind. As a result, you feel calm and refreshed.

1. Wear loose, comfortable clothing. Sit or lie in a relaxing position.
2. Close your eyes and concentrate on a calming thought, word or object.
3. You may find that other thoughts pop into your mind. Don't worry—this is normal. Try not to dwell on them. Just keep focusing on your image or sound.
4. If you're having trouble, try repeating a word or sound over and over. (Some people find it helpful to play soothing music while meditating.)
5. Gradually, you'll begin to feel more and more relaxed.

Deep breathing

One of the easiest ways to relieve tension is with deep breathing.

1. Lie on your back with a pillow under your head. Bend your knees (or put a pillow under them) to relax your stomach.
2. Put one hand on your stomach, just below your rib cage.
3. Slowly breathe in through your nose. Your stomach should feel like it's rising.
4. Exhale slowly through your mouth, emptying your lungs completely and letting your stomach fall.
5. Repeat several times until you feel calm and relaxed. Practice daily.

Once you are able to do this easily, you can practice this technique almost anywhere, at any time.

Notes

Use the space below to keep track of how these techniques work for you and any areas you want to improve on.

_____
_____
_____
_____
_____
_____
_____
_____
_____
_____
_____
_____
_____
_____
_____
_____
_____
_____
_____
_____

ALCOHOL AND OTHER DRUGS WON'T HELP.
Using alcohol, tobacco and other drugs can actually cause problems that may lead to even more stress.

Alcohol

Alcohol is a depressant and slows down the central nervous system.

- Alcohol may make some stressed—out people feel even worse.
- Heavy use can even lead to depression.

Limit alcohol—or don't drink at all. (People who should not drink at all include women who are pregnant or trying to get pregnant and people recovering from alcoholism.) Ask your health-care provider what's best for you. Also talk to him or her if you think you may have a problem with alcohol use.

Other drugs

Never use illegal drugs. If you do, get help to stop.

Tobacco

This contains nicotine, which is addictive. At first, it acts as a stimulant, but later it works as a depressant and tranquilizer. Smoking can cause lung cancer, heart disease and many other conditions. If you smoke or use other forms of tobacco, get help to quit. Your health-care provider can be a great resource for information on quitting.

If you take any medication for symptoms of stress, be sure to follow your health-care provider's advice exactly.

ASKING FOR HELP IS NOT A SIGN OF WEAKNESS.
It shows you are strong enough to admit you need help.
Getting professional help is smart!

If stress and its effects start to get out of hand, consider contacting:

Your health-care provider

He or she may suggest changes in your diet and activities, or prescribe medication. He or she may refer you to a therapist or counselor.

Your local hospital

Many hospitals offer stress management courses and sponsor support groups. Mental health centers These provide a variety of services, such as emergency help and outpatient treatment.

Employee Assistance Programs (EAPs)

Many employers offer these programs. An EAP can provide employees with referral or counseling for issues like drug and alcohol abuse, relationship problems or job stress.

State and local mental health associations

These organizations are good sources of information and advice on stress. If cost is a problem, they may be able to help you find care based on ability to pay.

Other professionals

Clergy, social workers, counselors and therapists, psychiatrists, psychologists or nurses can provide information on stress and help solve problems.

By working through the exercises in this workbook, you'll be able to target areas where these professionals can help.

DEVELOPING A STRESS MANAGEMENT PLAN

Now that you have greater insight into what causes your stress, how you respond to stressors and how you use your time, you can start developing a plan to bring stress under control. Follow these steps:

1. Set a goal and a time frame

Your goal should address both a specific behavior and your reaction. For example, over the next month, your goal could be to meditate whenever you feel stressed.

You may want to set more than one goal. That's OK, however, don't try to meet too many at one time—you could add to your stress.

2. Get support

Tell family, friends or co-workers about your goals. They can offer you encouragement.

3. Track your progress

Consider keeping a daily log as you move toward your goal. Seeing improvement over time can keep you from feeling discouraged.

4. Reward yourself

Treat yourself when you reach a goal or get halfway there. For example, go to a movie or enjoy a special meal.

Keep in mind that stress will not disappear just by reading this workbook. Relieving stress takes time. It's also an ever-changing process—stress-reducing techniques may work better for you than others. When your stress change, change your strategy for dealing with them, if necessary.

Commit to change.

Congratulations! Now that you've reached this point, you've probably uncovered some ideas to help you reduce stress. Pick the ones that will help you reach your goals, and make a plan to start practicing them. Don't forget to include a target date for reaching your goals. Good luck!

Goal	Plan of action	Target date
_____	_____	_____
_____	_____	_____
_____	_____	_____
_____	_____	_____
_____	_____	_____
_____	_____	_____
_____	_____	_____
_____	_____	_____
_____	_____	_____
_____	_____	_____
_____	_____	_____
_____	_____	_____
_____	_____	_____

My supporters: _____

Method of tracking progress: _____

Reward for meeting my goal(s): _____

_____

_____

Date _____ Your signature _____

Made in the USA
Columbia, SC
14 October 2024